THE PARISH CHURCHES OF LOUDOUN

AND THEIR CLERGY UP TO 1845.

PART 2

LOUDOUN PARISH CHURCH NEWMILNS

Alastair Hendry

2012

FOREWORD

In Part 1, I attempted to trace the early history of Loudoun Kirk, the original parish church of Loudoun, from its establishment in the late 12th century, and the development of the later chapel/church in Newmilns. Where possible, details of the officiating clergy were sought.

It was not long before I discovered that primary sources were few and far between and the secondary documentation, both old and more recent, was frequently inaccurate. Some of the generally accepted dates for a number of significant events are totally unsupported by documentary or physical evidence.

Part 2 takes the search from the transference of parochial status from Loudoun Kirk to the church in Newmilns in the 17th century up to the first clear dates to emerge in over six centuries – 3 May 1844 (laying of foundation stone of a new church) and 14 September 1845 (first service in the new church).

Where quotations are included, no attempt has been made to change the original spelling.

Alastair Hendry
December 2012

INTRODUCTION

The parish of Loudoun was developed within the boundaries of the grant of the lands of Loudoun, made in the late 12th century to James, son of Lambinus, by Richard de Moreville, Constable of Scotland and overlord of Cunningham in Ayrshire. James was the son of one of a group of Flemish incomers who had previously settled in Upper Clydesdale. The first parish church of Loudoun (Loudoun Kirk), situated at the western end of the parish probably dates from this early period (c.1188). Not long after its foundation, the revenues of Loudoun Kirk were appropriated to support the recently built Kilwinning Abbey and thus the Abbey became responsible for providing priests to care for the spiritual needs of the Loudoun parishioners.

Records of Loudoun Kirk's history are sparse. We can only guess at the effect of the wars of the 13th and 14th centuries on the little parish church, though we do have evidence that Kilwinning Abbey itself was badly affected and impoverished[1]. The earliest reference to a curate appointed by Kilwinning Abbey to minister at Loudoun Kirk occurs in the Vatican Records as late as 1465[2]. In 1527 the murder of Gilbert Kennedy, 2nd Earl of Cassillis, was attributed to the Sheriff of Ayr, Sir Hugh Campbell of Loudoun and his followers. The subsequent retaliation by the Kennedy faction brought destruction to Loudoun Castle, its woodlands and the nearby church[3]. Not long after the restoration of Loudoun Kirk, a chapel dedicated to the Blessed Virgin Mary was built in Newmilns around 1530, a recognition of the growing size and importance of the recently created free Burgh of Barony, as well as an increasing concentration of population some distance east of the more remote Loudoun Kirk, the parish church[4].

At the Reformation, both the original Loudoun Kirk to the west and the chapel in Newmilns became Protestant churches and were altered internally to conform to the new forms of religious observance. The chancel areas with their altars became redundant, as the emphasis in services focused on the preaching of the Word from the pulpit and the celebration of Communion, now participated in by the entire congregation at tables set up for the occasion. For almost a century, the two churches served the people of Loudoun, with the older Loudoun Kirk maintaining its status as the parish church.

LOUDOUN PARISH CHURCH IN NEWMILNS

By the early seventeenth century, the church in Newmilns had become the main focus for worship in the parish, perhaps made inevitable by the shift in population together with the construction of the Loudoun Family burial vault in the chancel area of the older Loudoun Kirk. Although one would expect over the centuries that repairs of all kinds would have to have been made to the church fabric, no documentary evidence exists for the construction of a new parish church building before the middle of the seventeenth century. It has been suggested in Part I that, probably in response to complaints about the existing church being in a ruinous condition and without a graveyard (noted as the result of a Presbytery visitation in 1649)[5] and lacking appropriate accommodation for the Earl of Loudoun and his family, extensive repair work was carried out and perhaps a new church built. It is interesting that almost at the same time (1650) the then minister, Mr John Nevay, came to a new and satisfactory agreement with the Earl of Loudoun on the size and nature of his stipend (five hundred merks in money and four chalders of meal and twelve bolls of barley, with the addition of four acres to his old glebe)[6]. The terms thus drawn up were destined to remain in force for 150 years much to the despair of later ministers.

The restored/rebuilt church in Newmilns where Mr Nevay and his congregation now worshipped would have been not massively different from the older building. Barn-like in appearance, the structure was rectangular with a starkly plain interior. Inside, set against the south wall was the pulpit, and beneath it the precentor's desk. Increasing numbers of members and the subsequent demand for more space necessitated the construction of one or more galleries or lofts on the east, west and north walls, access to which was by means of staircases. In many churches, these staircases were constructed outside against the church walls and entry to each gallery was through a door cut in the external wall. The area beneath the east gallery was frequently partitioned off for use, for example, as a schoolroom.

The central area of the church on Communion days was set out with tables and benches. At other times the congregation, for the most part, worshipped standing or sat on stools which they brought for their own use or obtained from the beadle. Pews became common a century later.

At some convenient point was situated the 'stool of repentance' or 'cutty stool' in full view of the assembled parishioners. Upon it sat, or stood, those who were guilty of some transgression and who had come to be harangued and rebuked at length and with full vigour by the minister on three consecutive Sundays in order to be absolved of their sin and so allowed to participate in the celebration of Communion. Over centuries and throughout Scotland, while the moral discipline of the congregations was vested in the care of the Kirk Sessions, the stools of repentance were in constant use.

Mr John Nevay, minister

From 1637, the incumbent at Newmilns was Mr John Nevay, a graduate of Aberdeen University and a man of considerable reputation for his strong principles and ready involvement in the work of the Kirk at national level. One writer describes him as 'a very zealous and honest though somewhat violent man, thrusting himself forward in all public questions'[7].

The documentary records of his activities suggest he spent much of his time in the public eye and had little time for the affairs of his parish. His involvement in the brutal slaughter of the surrendered garrison at Dunaverty in Kintyre in 1647 won for him the description of 'a bloody preacher' and lasting notoriety[8]. In 1648 he participated in the debacle at Mauchline Moor which resulted in his arrest, his later release and even later, when the political tide turned, his eventual exoneration[9].

On 31 July 1649, Mr Nevay was appointed a commissioner by Parliament for visiting the University of Aberdeen[10] and by January 1650 he was back on a new committee, this time charged with 'purging the Army of Malignant and scandalous persons'. He continued as an active member of the Commission of the Kirk, regularly attending meetings even at some distance from Loudoun, e.g. 28 November at Perth. When the Church divided into two factions, the resolutioners and protestors, he sided with the latter who were implacably opposed to Charles Stuart and demanded jurisdiction for the spiritual over civil matters. In 1654 he was selected by the Council of England to be a member of a committee for authorising admissions to the ministry in the area of the synod of Glasgow and Ayr. This was part of a policy aimed at establishing control over the type of individual entering the ministry. But Mr Nevay did not stay out of trouble for long.

Throughout his ministry, Mr Nevay's patron, John, the 1st Earl of Loudoun spent most of his time away from Loudoun, involved in national politics. On 1 January 1650, he had been present at Scone to witness the coronation of Charles II. Later that year he had been part of the Scottish army crushed by Cromwell's forces at Dunbar, and after the subsequent disaster at Worcester, he had withdrawn to the Highlands to join the Earl of Glencairn and other Royalists. As a result, when Cromwell was extending pardons to his former opponents in 1654, the Earl of Loudoun's name was not included. His estates were declared forfeit and the sum of £400, drawn from the estates, was settled on the Countess and his family[11]. He later surrendered to General Monck, made his peace and kept out of politics until the Restoration. He died on 15 March 1663 in Edinburgh, but was buried in the family vault in Loudoun Kirk.

In 1660, the high hopes in Church and State were dashed by the early legislation of Charles II. The Rescissory Act (1661)[12] repealed all legislation passed by parliaments since 1633. The episcopacy was reintroduced. Lay patronage was revived – ministers were to be presented by their patron and a bishop. The Covenants were declared unlawful and private conventicles forbidden. As synods and presbyteries could now meet only with the permission of the king and bishops, many ministers refused to attend. On 1 November 1662, those who refused to obey and attend were deprived of their charges. Mr Nevay was one of those who came immediately to notice.

'Information being given of the turbulent and seditious cariages (behaviour) and actings' of Mr Jon Neave and several other ministers, they were ordered to appear before the Privy Council at its next meeting in Edinburgh in December 1662[13]. Mr Nevay refused to take the oath of allegiance and was sentenced to be banished furth of his Majesty's dominions, being imprisoned in the tolbooth of Edinburgh until his departure. His promise to abide by the sentence was recorded as follows: 'I Mr Jon Neave, late minister at Newmilnes, binds and obliges me to remove myself furth of the Kinges dominions and not to return under paine of death, and that I shall remove before the first of February, and that I shall remain within the dioceses of Glasgow and Edinburgh in the meantyme. Subscribitur, Mr J Nevay'. It was countersigned by the Chancellor, the Marquis of Glencairn[14].

On 13 January 1663, Mr Nevay petitioned the Council for an extension to the time limit ' by reson of the shortnes of the tyme and tempestuous season of the winter tyme'. The Council replied with leniency and allowed him until 14 February 'to repair to any part or place for doeing his necessar affaires, provided he cary himself peaceably'[15]. Mr Nevay thereafter left for exile in Holland where he died some ten years later.

Mr William Hume, minister

His place was taken by William Hume, who came to Loudoun from the Borders. On 22 May 1648 he had been presented to Edrom parish by Charles I. But there is a question over whether he actually took up this charge as he appears to have been under scandal at the time. The presbytery of Chirnside was warned not to put him on the leet for any kirk until he had been tried and cleared[16]. He was translated to Ellem in the same presbytery in 1652, but in the following year on 17 March was admitted to Ayton. On June 1661, he petitioned Parliament, claiming that while he had been lawfully admitted to the church of Ayton in 1653, he had been 'violently bereft of his stipend for two years for his loyaltie and opposition to the remonstrateing partie'. It was decided that he should be reinstated and the arrears in stipend paid to him (2,400 merks Scots)[17]. Having conformed to Episcopacy, he was confirmed to this charge by Charles II on 4 October 1662 and collated 20 January 1663. A year later he was on the move and on 13 October 1664 he was translated to Loudoun[18].

His stay in Loudoun was short, however. He died in February 1666, leaving a wife and four children.

Not long after his death, the repression and persecution in SW Scotland ignited an uprising in November 1666 in Dumfries. The Dumfries rebels marched north into Ayrshire and were joined by many supporters, some from Loudoun. The force of some 2000 men under the command of Colonel Wallace of Dundonald marched east via Muirkirk, heading for Edinburgh. At Lanark, however, a large number of the marchers turned back, while the remainder continued on towards the capital. Tragically the support they had expected from the city and the surrounding district did not materialise and the depleted force was crushed at Rullion Green by General Thomas Hamilton of Dalziel[19]. John Nisbet of Hardhill who took part in the battle survived. Matthew Paton, a shoemaker in Newmilns, was taken prisoner and executed at Glasgow on 19 December 1666. David Findlay was shot at Newmilns by order of General Dalziel.

On July 1667 the Privy Council meeting in Edinburgh dealt with the petition of John Walker in Loudoun parish[20]. He had been a prisoner in the Cannongate 'upon suspition of accession to the late rebellion'. He pleaded innocence of the charge and, as proof of his remaining loyal, indicated that he was prepared to take 'the oath of allegiance and Declaration'. The Lords of Council accepted his oath and set him free 'to live peacably and loyally'.

Later the same month the Lords in Council, in order to secure the peace of the kingdom, appointed various noblemen, including the Earl of Loudoun, to visit their lands and 'requyre their men, tenents and servants to subscryve a band for their keeping the peace and releiving them of their ingagments'[21]. Anyone refusing to sign was to be disarmed and removed from his possessions, and those who continued to be disobedient were to be denounced as rebels and put to the horn. Another measure to preserve the peace was to settle militia in troubled areas of which Ayrshire was one. Again the Earl of

Loudoun was given the task of making the arrangements for his estates.

On 19 December 1668 order was given by the Privy Council that a force of seventy two foot soldiers of his Majesties regiment were to move west and quarter at Kilmarnock, Mauchline and Newmilns, twenty four of whom were to be billeted at the Earl's 'house of Newmilles' until further orders[22]. Six months later in 1669 they were moved to Glasgow to quarter there[23].

On 3 September 1672, faced with the growing menace of conventicles being held in the districts of the outed ministers, the Government decreed that certain of these ministers should be allowed to proceed to charges and parishes, often at a considerable distances from their own and 'to preach and exercise the other parts of their ministerial function'[24]. Strict conditions were laid down to cover their indulgence, including:

1. That they presume not to marry or baptise, except such as belong to the parish to which they are confined, or to the neighbouring parishes vacant or wanting ministers for the time.
2. That all ministers indulged in one and the same diocese, celebrate the communion upon one and the same Lord's day, and that they admit none to their communions belonging to other parishes, without testificates from the ministers thereof.
3. That they preach only in these kirks, and not in the church yards, nor any place else, under the pain to be reputed and punished as keepers of conventicles.

4. That they remain within, and depart not furth of, the parish to which they are confined, without licence from the bishop of the diocese only.
5. That in the exercise of discipline, all such cases as were formerly referable to presbyteries, continue still in the same manner; and where there is no presbyterial meeting, that these cases be referred to the presbytery of the next bounds.
6. That the ordinary dues payable to bursars, clerks of presbyteries and synods, be paid by the same ministers as formerly.[25]

Mr John Burnet, who had been minister at East Kilbride and Torrens parish church from 1656, and Mr George Campbell, minister at Dumfries, both of whom had been deprived in 1662, were indulged to Loudoun on 3 September 1672[26]. Neither man was prepared to accept this move. Mr Burnet continued to refuse and died on 22 December 1673, aged about 57. Mr Campbell evaded arrest until 1684, and on his later release fled to Holland. He returned to Dumfries in 1687 and was restored to the First Charge there on 25 April 1690. He died on 3 July 1701[27].

On 10 July 1673, the troops quartered in the parishes of Old and New Kilmarnock were removed and quartered in the town of Newmilns, to be supplied with grass collected from the parishes of Loudoun and Galston[28].

Mr Hugh Campbell, minister

The records of the Church of Scotland show that Mr Hume was followed by a Mr Hugh Campbell around 1673. The details of his involvement with Loudoun are not clear, if indeed there was any. Mr Campbell, a graduate of Glasgow University in 1654, was minister of Muirkirk. He was one of the ministers outed in 1662, but confined to his parish. At some time therafter, possibly 1673, he was indulged to Loudoun, but if so his stay must have been very short.

On 9 March 1675, as they had been found not guilty of keeping conventicles, Mr Hugh Campbell and several others were to receive their stipends from the respective kirks at which they preached, and that for the year 1674 and for all the preceding years still owing[29]. It is not certain if this Hugh Campbell is the one referred to in the records. He was ordered to be summoned on 15 July 1675, for baptising and marrying irregularly, and on 15 June 1676 for preaching at Muirkirk without a presentation[30]. He appeared before the Council and was ordered, before the second Thursday of July next to get presentation (from the patron) and collation (from the bishop) to the said kirk, or else he would have to face the charges. In 1678, his life was in considerable danger at the hands of extremist covenanters who violently opposed indulgences granted to ministers, but their plans were thwarted through the agency of James, Earl of Loudoun. Mr Campbell was allowed to return to his charge in Muirkirk in 1687, where he continued in service until his death in 1714[31].

Mr Antony Shaw, minister

Around 1674, Mr Antony Shaw was translated to Loudoun parish. A graduate of Edinburgh University (17 April 1639), he had been licensed by the Presbytery of Stranraer on 12 March 1645 and ordained the following year as minister to a Presbyterian congregation in Belfast. In January 1650, he was admitted to the charge of Colmonell in south Ayrshire. During his time there he married Agnes, the sister of Fergus M'Cubbin, the laird of Knockdolian. They had a son, Fergus, and a daughter Margaret. He was deprived of his charge in 1662. On 3 September 1672, he was appointed under indulgence to Paisley. Two years later he came to Loudoun[32].

His time there did not run smoothly. After a year's service, he, like quite a number of other ministers in Ayrshire, had not been paid and had to petition to the Privy Council to persuade the heritors to see to their stipends[33].

In 1677, trouble of a different kind in Loudoun[34]. John Frow in the Mill of Newmilns complained to the Privy Council that 'Upon the cruell threatenings of Murdoch Loudoune, younger in Newmilnes, Alexander Lowdoune at Lowdounmilnes, Agnes Finlay his spouse, Marjorie Loudoun, his daughter, and Janet Loudoune, his sister, to give the petitioner and his familie ane hott kalkening, and such lyke expressiones, ther haveing in Appryll last happened ane sudden fyre near to the petitioner's dwelling house. whereby the same was set on fyre and his barne, stable and byre adjoining therto burnt to ashes and the petitioner and his family scarcely saved, the said fyve persones, upon their saids former expressiones, renewed that same night of the fyre and other presumptiones such as being furth of their bedds the tyme the fyre begane, and some of them being seine carrying burnt peets alongst the streets at the very tyme, wer apprehended and being brought before the bailzies of Newmilnes, they, as conscious of their guilt and fearing to byde a tryall, did voluntarly banish themselves furth of the kingdome and by bond enacted themselves never to return therto under the payne of death'. Unfortunately the accused fireraisers now threatened to return and do the petitioner and his family further mischief. The Privy Council ordered that, should they return to Scotland, they must be immediately arrested.

On 29 January 1678, the Privy Council met at Glasgow and, in the face of civil unrest, initiated moves for the disarming of all inhabitants of Ayrshire, from the heritors to their servants[35]. All were instructed to appear at their parish kirk or kirktoun, e.g. Loudoun on 13 February and Galston on the 15th, and bring with them 'their armes of all sortes, such as musketts, pistolls, swords, pickes, halberts, Lochaber axes, durkes and whingers'. Noblemen and gentlemen of quality were allowed to retain the privilege of wearing their swords. Public announcements of the arrangements for the disarming were to be made in the parishes and at market crosses.

At a meeting in Ayr on 9 February 1678, further requirements were made that all and sundry, heritors, liferenters, landlords, magistrates and councillors of burghs sign a bond that they would attend at the tolbooth in Ayr and agree to the methods being put in place to secure the peace and quiet of the country and to preserve it from 'disorders' in the future. The date for the appearance of the parishioners of 'Lowdoun and newmilles' was the 21st February. Public intimation of this information was to be made at the parish kirks upon a Sabbath after divine service. The Earl of Loudoun refused to sign the bond, but, when summoned, he denied it, explaining that he had been prevented by his wife's illness. The Committee freed him of the charge[36]. Despite this, later that year (1678) the Earl's name appeared on another list of those who had not signed the bond and orders were given for them to be arrested and sent to the tolbooths of Ayr, Irvine or Glasgow[37].

In March 1678, James, Earl of Loudoun, and other noblemen, who had been appointed commissioners of excise for Ayrshire, were summoned and criticised for not meeting with their fellow commissioners to set rates and prices 'both upon mens meat and horse meat' for the use of the garrisons stationed in Ayrshire. They were ordered to proceed to their task without further delay[38].

In 1679, continuing trouble in the parish of Loudoun. Local opposition to the troops stationed there resulted in the killing of two soldiers and the wounding of several others. The Earl of Loudoun 'who hes the most considerable interest in that place and on whose ground it was done' was ordered to attend the Privy Council 'to give a full representation and discovery of that mater upon his alledgeance'[39]. This incident took place against the background of growing discontent, the reports of 'strong and armed conventicles in many distant places' and activities of the local population which 'hinder the inbringing of his Majesties ces (taxes)'.

Not long afterwards, James, the 2nd Earl of Loudoun, a strong supporter of the Covenanters, was forced to go into exile in Holland. Even so, he still maintained contact with his with and family at Loudoun. From him the people of Loudoun received the gift of a 'passing bell'. Also called a 'deid bell' or a 'skellet bell', this bell was for use at funerals. The bell-ringer travelled round the district letting the people know of an individual's passing and later led the funeral cortege to the kirkyard. The bronze bell had the words 'LOUDOUN KIRK' cast in raised lettering upon it. The Earl never returned to Loudoun. He died at Leyden in 1684[40].

On 1 June 1679, news of a large conventicle being held at Drumclog reached the authorities. Graham of Claverhouse with three troops of cavalry rushed to disperse it and arrest the leaders. Many of the Covenanters, however, had come armed and the Government troops were overwhelmed. Two days later a royal proclamation criticised these 'disloyall persons, who have formerly tasted our royall bounty and clemency' and described how after Drumclog the rebels pursued and continued to assault the Government troops as far as and into Glasgow; 'and have seized upon the persons of diverse our good subjects, plundered and robbed them of their horses, arms and other goods, and have done and committed many other outrages and treasonable deeds and attempts against our authority…'[41]. Several men of Loudoun perished during or after the battle, including John Gebbie in Feoch and John Morton in Broomhill (commemorated in Loudoun churchyard, Newmilns) and Thomas Fleming of Loudounhill (memorial stone beside Loudoun Kirk). Captain John Nisbet of Hardhill and John Morton, the Darvel blacksmith, survived.

The defeat at Drumclog prompted an even more vigorous response from the Government. A more powerful force was despatched under the command of James, Duke of Monmouth, Charles II's illegitimate son. They caught up with the Covenanters at Bothwell Brig and completely crushed them. Some 1400 prisoners were taken to Edinburgh and penned up in Greyfriars Churchyard to await punishment[42]. Of the Loudoun men taken at or after Bothwell Brig, James Wood was executed. Some 257 other prisoners were sentenced to banishment to America and packed aboard a vessel, the 'Crown of London' lying at Leith. The ship carrying them hit rocks in a storm off Muil Head of Durness, Orkney on 10 December 1679 and foundered. As the hatches had been battened down to make sure no-one escaped, 209 Covenanters perished. Only 48 escaped when the hull split open on the rocks. 59 of those on board were from half the parishes in Ayrshire. Of these unfortunates, 52 perished and 7 survived[43]. A mystery surrounds the one man from Loudoun, Thomas Wylie. In all the published lists he is listed among the dead. But in the Register of the Privy Council for 31 July 1679, an order is recorded releasing one Thomas Wylie, a 'tenant to the Earl of Loudoun' being held in Greyfriars Kirkyard, because he had signed a bond promising not take up arms again[44]. This was more than four months before the ill-fated 'Crown of London' set sail from Leith. A mistake in the lists? Two or three Thomas Wylies (there was another Thomas Wylie from Stewarton who perished)? The problem remains unsolved.

The repression which followed upon Bothwell Brig became even more severe. The main Covenanting movement had been crushed, but a small number of extremists led by Richard Cameron carried on the struggle until he and his small force were defeated at Airds Moss near Muirkirk in 1680[45]. A search for rebels extended throughout the southwest of Scotland. From their headquarters in the tower house in Newmilns, the Government troops scoured the countryside. Covenanters found were summarily shot or imprisoned to await trial. About three dozen perished in Ayrshire. These were the Killing Times[46]. Among those whose names we know were John Nisbet in Glen executed at Kilmarnock in 1683 and James Nisbet in Highside who suffered the same fate at Glasgow a year later. Captain John Nisbet of Hardhill, a local hero who had survived Rullion Green, Drumclog and Bothwell Brig and had a reward of £2,000 placed on his head, was betrayed, taken to Edinburgh and executed there in the Grassmarket on 4 December 1685[47].

On occasion the actions of the Government soldiers exhibited a terrible barbarity. James White in Fenwick was executed by Captain Inglis and his men. His head was brought back to Newmilns and used as a football by the soldiers on the town green. Newmilns tower house was used as a billet for the soldiers and also as a temporary prison. It was here that the Covenanters, arrested by Captain Inglis at Little Blackwood farm in Kilmarnock parish in April 1685, were lodged prior to execution. A group of their friends staged a rescue attempt by smashing their way into the prison and killing a guard. All eight prisoners escaped, but one of their rescuers, John Law, was shot and killed by a soldier firing from the tower parapet[48].

While the government troops sought to control the activities of rebels in SW Scotland in 1683, attempts were being made at a national level to stimulate trade and commerce. One industry of particular concern was the manufacture of cloth necessary for making uniforms for the soldiers[49]. The monopoly for supplying such materials was given to the weavers of Newmilns, despite the parish's reputation as a hotbed of rebellion. Unfortunately it quickly became clear that their output was insufficient to meet demand. The Privy Council gave the owners of the business permission (contrary to their normal trade policy) to import specific additional amounts of cloth at specified prices from England. This meant a great deal of time and trouble for the agents who had to check and mark these special imports. The business in Newmilns struggled. Because of unexpected costs of hiring extra skilled foreign workers and of buying in the extra materials required for the preparation of the cloth, such as oil, dyes, etc., the owners petitioned the Privy Council that they be allowed to import these materials free of duty. There was also the problem of other merchants, especially in Edinburgh, breaching the Newmilns' monopoly by illegally importing English cloth and selling it at lower prices. To make matters even worse the army expected its totally unrealistic demands for the cloth to be met immediately[50].

On 2 August 1683, Mr Shaw was summoned before the Court of Justiciary in Edinburgh for the crime of preaching at a field conventicle in the churchyard of

Colmonell[51]. His plea indicated that participation in the conventicle was highly imprudent and he was very sorry. 'He had no evill designe therein nor wes he disaffected to his Majestie or his government, but, upon the contrare, takes God to witnes that he still prayed privatly and publictly for his Majesties welfare and the welfare of all the royall familie, and wes still againest all ryseing in armes againest his Majestie and the government upon any pretence whatsoever, upon which account it is nottourlie known to the haill countrie where he lives that he wes most cruellie hunted after and threatned by the rebells in the late rebellion in the year 1679, and declaires coram Deo he never wished nor prayed for successe to these rebells'. He explained also that he was 'a poor, infirm man past sixty four yeirs of age subject to gravell, seeatick, and presentie in the hazard of his life by these and other diseases in this intemperat season'. He asked the Council to treat him with compassion. The Council revoked his indulgence to preach, declared the kirk of Loudoun vacant and ordered him to find caution not to preach or act as minister under the penalty of five thousand merks, or else leave the kingdom altogether[52]. He was put in prison until the guarantees could be found. Within days a new petition was submitted to the Council by Janet Taylor, Mr Shaw's (second) wife. She maintained that her husband 'being an old man near seventy years and by age and infirmity brought very low, and by his restraint in all humane appearance in great danger of his life', in addition to the fact that she was a 'poor gentlewoman having little to maintain her husband and her familie and not in a condition to bear the expense in attending him here, and she being desireous of nothing more in the world then to be present with and oversee her husband now in his great distresse and near his expireing'. The Council acceded to her request, freed her husband on the guarantee that he would never again 'keep conventicles in house or feild, nor baptize nor marry, but shall demain himselfe peaceably and loyaly and be a regular hearer and frequenter of the publict worship in the paroch kirk where shall happen to reside, under the penalty of five thousand merks in caise of faylie'[53].

After a career of some forty years in the ministry, Mr Shaw's health began to deteriorate rapidly. He suffered severe nasal haemorrhages and was dead by 20 September 1687. He was survived by his wife, his son Fergus and daughter Margaret. Not long afterwards, his wife, 'a lady, eminent for her piety, skill in physic and long experience,' succumbed to the same illness as her late husband[54].

When the Presbytery records begin again in 1687, the Loudoun charge was still vacant and the minister's preaching duties at least were being covered by pulpit supply. On 2 May 1688, the Call was to be made to a Mr James Brown, the Presbytery letter 'shewing their hearty concurring and pressing his hearkning to that Call'[55].

Mr James Brown was no stranger to the parish of Loudoun. His father was Nicol Brown, an officer of dragoons who had settled in Newmilns and married a daughter of Brown of Ranoldcoup in Darvel. During the troubled times of Charles II's reign, Mr Brown took refuge in America (1685). Despite many invitations to remain in that country and take pastoral charge over one or other of its districts, he was welcomed back to Newmilns two years later. His past then caught up with him and he was summoned to appear before the Court of Justiciary in Edinburgh on 6 April 1688 on charges of involvement in 'the rebellion at Bothwell Bridge (22 June 1679), harbouring, recepting, conversing with, and doing favours to rebells and traitors and other treasonable crymes'. The case was dismissed and he was freed. Not long afterwards came the Call from Loudoun. Mr Brown, however, after consideration, gave preference to a Call to Glasgow. For many years thereafter he was minister of the High Church of that city, serving for a time as Dean of Faculty in the College of Glasgow[56].

Later that year (1688) the parishioners of Loudoun were asking not only for continuing help in finding a minister but also for promoting 'the choise of some persons in thir parish for assisting in the more orderly and effectual managing of the affairs of the parish especially in order to the plantation (of a minister)'[57]. On 29 August a 'list of fitt persons to be elders' was ready to be intimated to the congregation and arrangements made for their ordination to make up the numbers on the depleted kirk session.

Mr John Campbell, minister

On 16 April 1689, the Earl of Loudoun recommended that a Mr John Campbell (who was attending Presbytery) be asked to supply the parish of Newmilns 'as long as he may convenientlie and promising what incouradgement to him can be expected'. Mr Campbell agreed to help until the next

Presbytery meeting[58]. A grateful Presbytery thanked the Earl and Mr Campbell, who went on to act as supply for much of that year, with the popular support of the parishioners. Indeed, it may be that he had been acting as pulpit supply since Mr Shaw's death. However, there was a problem. Mr John Campbell was a Conformist in a Presbytery of non-Conformist ministers. In September 1689, two representatives of the Presbytery conferred with Mr Campbell and reported 'that he gave them ane short account of his lyfe and Conformitie, and was ready to acknowledge his offence in Conforming and taking the Test'. Further discussion had to be undertaken with him because of the seriousness of the matter to some of the Presbytery. They felt that this was also necessary 'especiallie since he is to remove to the highlands and seek a recommendation from this presbytery'[59]. As Mr Campbell's intended departure was well known, the heritors, elders and parishioners gained permission to call Mr John Campbell, minister of Carncastle in Ireland to be their minister[60]. There now followed more than five years of a somewhat strange involvement of this Mr Campbell with the parish and Presbytery. Firstly, he never accepted the Call, and was never given permission by his Presbytery of Antrim to do so. Yet he lived in Newmilns with his family presumably in the manse and acted as minister. The Conformist Mr Campbell's note of demission was rejected, because the Presbytery were not 'satisfied with the fulnes and forme of it', and he was told to rewrite it in a more appropriate fashion[61]. On 5 February 1690, his formal demission was accepted and engrossed in the Presbytery minutes. 'The Tenor wherof was as follows: I Mr Johne Campbell having officiat for several yeares as the Conformist minister of the parish of Loudoun, and being now convinced of, and truely grieved for diverse failyeouris in the way of my entrie to the foirsaid charge .... by these presentis I doe actuallie dimitt and passe from anie relation I would be supposed to have to that people, and am content and doe consent that the said parish be declared vacant by these to whom it is competent so to doe to that I doe earnestlie desire the Reverend ministers of the presbyterian persuasion within the presbytery of Irvine, in whose bounds the said parish lyes, to contribute their pious endeavours for having that parish supplied with a faithfull Gospel minister in a way aggreable to their oune principalls and most conducive to the edification of that flock'[62]. Later on 25 March the Presbytery were pleased to provide another recommendation for him to assist his move to a charge in the Presbytery of Jedburgh.

The 'Irish' John Campbell continued to live in Newmilns, served as minister (without responding to the original Call) and attended the Presbytery meetings. The Presbytery and the Earl of Loudoun wrote repeatedly to Antrim for them to 'declare Mr John Campbell transportable'. On 28 October 1690, he was sufficiently a member of Presbytery that he was asked 'to prech at Finnick the next tuesday and to declare that Kirk vacant'. But the Presbytery of Antrim steadfastly refused to part with their colleague. At Newmilns, it would appear that not everyone approved. At the meeting in Irvine of 24 February 1691, a parishioner from Newmilns 'tainted with divisive and separating principles appeared'. It was reported that 'he had a paper in the name of the rest of the separation in that parish to give in against

Mr Campbell's Call'. Such dissension was quickly quashed. Contact with Antrim continued, and indeed on occasion Mr Campbell visited his neglected charge in Carncastle but returned to his family and parishioners in Newmilns. In November 1691, he received a certificate testifying to the fact that for the year past he had exercised his ministry at Loudoun at the desire of the people and appointment of the presbytery'[63]. A month later, however, Mr Campbell left Loudoun and returned to Carncastle. The search for a minister began again. The charge was vacant throughout 1692, 1693, 1694 and 1695.

In the midst of the previous search, the Presbytery also concerned itself with some of the more mundane matters of the parish. On 9 August 1688, James Findlay in Riccarton, who had previously promised marriage to Margaret Morton in Newmilns but had clearly realised that the relationship had foundered, dissolved the agreement and declared that she was now free to marry whom and when she pleased[64].

Two months later it was reported by a supply minister that a James Richmond 'had kept two children for a considerable time from baptism'. Robert Nisbet, an elder, was despatched to deal with the backslider and 'to make him sensible of his contemning of the ordinance of baptism'[65]. Once he had publicly acknowledged his sin before the congregation, he could have his children baptised. But James Richmond moved faster than Presbytery justice. After a year, it was reported that he was no longer in the parish and no-one knew where he had gone.

On 2 July 1689, a collection throughout the Presbytery for 'the indigent French and Ireland protestants now in this kingdom' raised the sum of almost £710, of which Newmilns contributed £21[66]. In 1693, the parishioners were less generous. A collection on behalf of poor scholars within their bounds produced no response or money from Loudoun.

At the beginning of 1691, the old familiar problem was being dealt with. 'John Mair of Little Loudownhill haveing faln in adultery with Janet Lambie then his servant did compeir 13 Sabbath Dayes publickly before the Congregation of Loudown upon the repentant stooll and was absolved according to order by the minister Mr John Campbell and Session on the 18 of januarij 1691 had his bastard baptized called Hugh the 29 Day of the forsaid moneth.' This and another item was inserted among the list of marriages after 1753 in the Old Parish Register of Loudoun, perhaps the copy of information contained in the missing Kirk Session records[67].

Another problem of a parish served by supply ministers was highlighted after Mr Campbell's departure. Several children in the parish had not been baptised 'because the parents either slighted or neglected to tak the opportunitie of having the ordinance of baptism administered to their children quhen the presbytery sent supplie unto them'. Not only that, one of the elders had been caught working 'one of the Last fast days it being in the time of the harvest and there being no minister there to preach to the people quhich scandall is not yet removed'. All elders were exhorted to persuade the parents to see to getting their children baptised forthwith. The guilty elder was to be rebuked in the Kirk Session, and a minister was to preach to the congregation and 'give a warning to others to bewarr of the sik practise in time comeing'.[68]

At national level, the departure of James VII and the coming of William of Orange to the throne, at last opened up the way for presbyterianism to finally achieve supremacy in Scotland. In the years that followed the Church in Scotland could operate freely in a manner only hoped for a century before.

Locally in Loudoun, the Presbytery and the Earl of Loudoun were still failing to identify a possible successor to Mr Campbell. On 21 May 1695, however, the Earl wrote to the Presbytery informing them of a likely candidate in the Presbytery of Glasgow. He urged them to contact that body 'that they would allow Mr Fawside to come and supply Newmilnes a day or two, as also a letter might be written to the young man himselfe that the business be the more effectuall all which the Presbytery agreed to and appointed this much to be signified to Loudoun'[69]. Mr Hugh Fawside, son of a Glasgow merchant and a graduate of Glasgow University, attended the meeting of Presbytery in Irvine on 9 July and was given the exercise of delivering a sermon at the next meeting on John 14,1. This he did successfully. On 27 August he delivered his 'Common Head' in English before the people, and was required to preach a sermon the following day on 1 Peter 2, 3. The common head to the Presbytery was conducted in Latin ('de purgatorio') and followed by 'language and questionary trials'. In all he was approved.[70]

Mr Hugh Fawside (Fauside, Fawsyde), minister

On 18 September 1695, Mr Hugh Fawside was 'solemnly ordained and sett apairt to the work of the ministry att Lowdoun .... and was unanimously received by the Heritors and Elders of the place.' It was recommended to the Heritors 'to see to **the reparation of the Church and manse which are now owt of case**, which they readily promised to do, as also every other thing for the Comfort and encouradgement of Mr Fawside their minister'.[71]

Mr Fawside was to devote his entire ministry to the people of Loudoun. On 31 January 1701, he married Lilias Weir, the daughter of a Glasgow surgeon.[72] The marriage was blessed with a son James (b. 20 December 1706) and three daughters, Kathrine (b. 8 November 1702), Christian (b. 26 February 1705, who in November 1730 married Mr John Campbell, minister of Muirkirk and later of the neighbouring parish of Galston) and Lillias (c. 31 December 1708). After the death of Lilias, his first wife, Mr Fawside married secondly Margaret Campbell on 2 October 1710. He married thirdly Margaret Hamilton, daughter of Captain Hamilton of Ladyland, on 30 April 1716. They had a daughter, Elizabeth (c. 29 October 1717).[73]

The fact that the kirk session records for this period have not survived means that we lack direct evidence of the session's work in the parish. Fortunately, however, Mr Fawside's reports to the presbytery of

Irvine help to illustrate some of the session's major concerns. Indeed, a clear illustration of the nature of kirk session work is shown in the list of questions drawn up at the Presbytery meeting of 11 June 1723[74], which were put forward as appropriate for the times when the session met to submit themselves to 'censure'.

1. do ye visit the sick in your division (district), speak to them and pray with them when ye are called?
2. do ye inform yourself of the Conversation (behaviour) of your division, particularly whether they have family worship and attend ordinances?
3. do ye give account of what Scandals fall out, which deserve publick censure?
4. do ye deal with their Conscience, who are guilty of such Escapes as do not deserve to be Represented to the Session?
5. do ye deal with persons under Scandal to bring them to repentance?
6. do ye attend Judicatory as ye can conveniently?
7. do ye make Conscience to rule your own family well, Worshipping God in it twice a day, Instruct your family and Endeavour to give them a good Example?
8. do ye visit your Division every half year and see whether Strangers have brought Testimonials?
9. (for Deacons) do ye Enquire into the state of the poor and Represent their Condition to the Session?

To judge from the number of references in the Presbytery records, the major concern of Mr Fawside and the kirk session was the sexual misbehaviour of a number of the parishioners, and it must be remembered that the cases brought to the notice of the Presbytery were a fraction of the total number and only those deemed the most serious or intractable.

On 12 December 1710 William Aird in Cronan, who had committed adultery with Elizabeth Brown, sometime his servant (who had given birth to their child and then murdered it), and been 'laid under sentence of greater excommunication', appealed for the sentence to be lifted[75]. He had been repentant and responded to the moral guidance of the session. After publicly, before the congregation of Loudoun, confessing his guilt and expressing his awareness of the depth of his sin, he was gravely and seriously admonished by Presbytery. Permission was given for him to be absolved.

In some cases, presbyteries and kirk sessions communicated with each other when individuals tried to escape their attention. On 12 June 1712 the kirk session of Dundonald met and heard a report of one Marion Patrick, who had attended Communion in the church there and then the following Monday committed adultery with a corporal of Captain Rodger's Dragoons[76]. Rather than face the session, she had absconded. The minister was tasked to examine the affair further and try to determine where she had fled to, so that the minister of that parish might be contacted with a view to her being returned to Dundonald. On 17 July, the minister reported that she had been traced to Newmilns and the session there had demanded her return to her own parish. Marion Patrick was present that day and answered the questions put to her, much to the dismay of the session. They postponed any decision until a later meeting when witnesses would be called. At that meeting on 7 September, the appearance of the witnesses clearly shook her and when tackled by a small group of the session, she confessed herself guilty of 'the sin of uncleanness' with the dragoon. But she refused to acknowledge that she had committed adultery. At the same time she asked the proceedings to be deferred to the end of the harvest lest she lose her earnings. The session agreed to do this. In December, she was again summoned, rebuked for the sin of adultery, and ordered to appear before the Presbytery of Ayr on 31 December. The Presbytery found that they could not pursue the dragoon as the unit had been disbanded and all of them had gone home to England. Marion Patrick by this time had disappeared and was declared 'fugitive from discipline' and this was to be intimated from the pulpit the following Sunday[77].

At the Presbytery meeting in Kilmarnock on 14 February 1734, Mr Fawside brought in a report on John Richmond and Janet Gilchrist in the parish of Loudoun guilty together of fornication. This was the fourth time he was so guilty and her third. They appeared and confessed their guilt and were rebuked, and exhorted to repent, and because of the 'attrociousness' of their sin (she having already been under the sentence of the greater excommunication upon the 'presumptions proven of her designed murder of her own child and absolved, and he now again guilty with her at the time when he was applying for absolution from the lesser excommunication) they were unanimously put under the sentence of the greater excommunication. This sentence was not only to show the church's abhorrence of what they had done but 'for terror to others and the awakening of them the more to a sense of their great sin'[78].

Some cases took up an inordinate amount of the Presbytery's time and attention, often because of the obduracy of those involved. In November 1711 Mr Fawside reported on the case of James Richmond and Margaret Cuthbertson accused of adultery[79]. He had confessed, but claimed that he had been 'fuddled and senselessly drunk'. She was a well-known character, who was 'infamous for Whoredom' and had been expelled from Kilmarnock for that reason. Despite the fact that the couple had been discovered in flagrante delicto by witnesses, Richmond revoked his confession and pleaded not guilty. All the evidence was collected and mulled over over a period of two years before it was decided to excommunicate him[80].

The Presbytery records also shed a little light on some of the tasks undertaken by Mr Fawside. In July 1711, he was appointed with a colleague and tradesmen to inspect Kilwinning Church, identify the repairs necessary and prepare a detailed list of essential expenditure[81]. Collections for various pressing causes had to be organised, e.g. a contribution from his own stipend to be used for 'repressing Popery in the North'[82], and parish collections for propagating the Gospel in Pennsylvania (£4 from Loudoun out of a total of over £48 sterling)[83] or for the suffering Protestants in Lithuania (£8 8s out of £29 16s 6d from the whole Presbytery)[84]. Mr Fawside also took his turn at the 'Exercise' in Presbytery and his preaching on Ephesians 5, 32 ('This is a great Mysterie') was approved[85]. He was selected as the Presbytery's Commissioner to the General Assembly in 1722 and 1726.

The threat of Catholicism was ever present and appeared at different levels. Among the instructions provided for Commissioners to the General Assembly in 1712 was one for 'ministers to take special care of Instructing their people in the principles of our Holy religion and to acquaint them with the abomination of popery and superstition'[86]. On 9 February 1714 concerns were being expressed in Presbytery of the 'restless endeavours of a Jacobite party to advance the Interest of a popish pretender in the face of standing Laws' and a day for publick fasting and humiliation fixed because of it[87]. Again in December, another presbyterial fast was fixed as a result of the many heinous sins arising form the fact that 'our Inveterate Enemy, a malignant popish and Jacobite party' had been allowed 'to proclaim their wicked designs against our Religion and Country'[88]. When it was reported that there was a 'Popish servant' in the household of the Earl of Eglinton, the Presbytery immediately insisted that she be dismissed[89]. The Earl replied that he thought that the Presbytery should have checked that the information was accurate and that she was a catholic. It was said also that 'she argued for popish principles and did not wait upon public ordinances' (did not attend church services). They desired his Lordship not to keep her in his service. And indeed later it was reported the the girl had left the Earl's service.

In 1716, Mr Fawside was chosen as Moderator of the Presbytery for the ensuing half year. During this time he brought up a topic which clearly he felt very strongly about – patronage. Patronage in the Church had been a subject of controversy since both The First Book of Discipline and The Second Book of Discipline had unsuccessfully called for its abolition. Though abolished in 1649, it was fully restored in 1712. It was the practice therefore, when there was a vacant charge, for the patron of the parish to present a candidate for the approval of the congregation. That November the representative of Mr William Blair Younger of that Ilk presented Mr John Fullartoun, a probationer, to be minister of Dalry. The documentation was brought to Mr Fawside, as Moderator, at his dwelling in Newmilns and read to those present by Mr Alexander Stevenson, the Irvine minister. Witnesses were Robert Steel in Burnmouth of Loudoun, Hugh Mason, his servant, and John Henderson, Mr Fawsides's servant. But after this business, Mr Fawside, 'the Moderator Remonstrated against Patronage as a grievance to this Church. And protested against this presentation for the presbyteries right, alledging that the power of presenting to the said Church was fallen into the presbyteries hand'[90]. Arrangements were then made for Mr Fullartoun to go to Dalry and preach a number of Sundays. Thereafter Mr Fawside would hold a session meeting to find out 'the inclinations of the Elders and others with respect to this affair'. Mr Fullartoun was later, in April 1717, ordained and inducted as minister of Dalry.

The matter did not end there. At its meeting on 1 January 1717, patronage was again high on the agenda[91]. There was a general consensus with regard to 'the grievous burden that patronage is to this Church and that this Presbyterie hath suffered more thereby than any other presbyterie since the Late Act of Parliament thereanent. It was Represented that it might be expedient to draw up a Memorial of the bad usage thereof by patrons in the bounds of this presbyterie since that time and to send the same to the two Ministers Professor Hamilton and Mr Mitchell at Edinburgh who are appointed by the Commission of the General Assembly to go to London to waite upon the King and Parliament for Redress of this Grievance'.

What of Mr Fawside's relationship with his own patrons, Hugh, the 3rd and John the 4th Earls of Loudoun? The records are puzzling. The 3rd Earl had played various important roles in national politics, e.g. in the drawing up of the Treaty of Union (1707) and as Scottish Representative Peer for twenty four years until his death at Loudoun Castle in 1731. He also acted as Lord High Commissioner to the Church of Scotland six times between 1722 and 1731. For his continued support in the affairs of the Church, the Presbytery of Irvine frequently appointed groups of its members to wait upon the Earl when he was in residence at Loudoun Castle. On only one occasion during his entire fifty seven year ministry was Mr Fawside included in one of these groups. That was on 8 May 1730, and even then that visit had to be abandoned because the Earl was abroad.

Occasionally in these records, reference is made to natural phenomena. There was no meeting of the Presbytery on 26 September 1712[92], because 'there was the greatest Land flood of any which had been seen for many years past'. On the other hand, on 13 July 1714, anxiety was being expressed over the danger to fruits from 'a great Excessive Drought'[93]. In 1720, there were anxieties of a different kind arising from 'flagrant reports of the plagues Invading the Isle of Man and so the imminent danger that we in these bounds are in by reason of frequent tradeing with that place'[94]. All of these events activated days of 'solemn Humiliation, Fasting and Prayer'.

At the meeting in Irvine on 9 March 1737, Mr Fawside's apologies for non-attendance were presented as well as the report that Communion which was normally celebrated twice in the year in the summer and October, had not been celebrated at all during the preceding year 'because of the distressed condition of his family'. The Presbytery noted and accepted his excuse[95].

A NEW CHURCH BUILDING IN NEWMILNS?

Dr Norman Macleod, a later minister of Loudoun Parish, in his 1842 report for the New Statistical Account of Scotland indicated with confidence that the parish church in Newmilns was built in 1738. A stone built high up into the south wall of the modern Loudoun Parish Church bears the date 1738 and seems to suggest that Dr Macleod was correct. But so far the search for documentary proof of this date has failed to confirm that claim. The church and manse had been brought up to an acceptable standard in preparation for the arrival of Mr Fawside in 1695. This was normal practice for new incumbents. Reference is also made in the Presbytery of Irvine records of improvements made to the manse in 1708 and 1724. But none to the building of the church in 1738. In 1791, Dr George Lawrie, the then minister, did not indicate any date for its construction in his evidence to the Old Statistical Account[97]. In his account he only stated that 'the church is new and in good repair.' In the absence of kirk session records, what evidence do the Presbytery records provide on this matter?

On 13 March 1750[98], at the meeting of Presbytery in Irvine, a petition was presented on behalf of Mr Fawside claiming that both kirk and manse were 'in a ruinous condition' and requested that a visitation be arranged to examine the situation. 'Both Church and Manse are so extremely insufficient', he wrote, 'that it is notoriously known to be dangerous to attend divine worship in the One And your Petitioners Family is in perpetual hazard by dwelling in the other, so that any delay in granting this Petition will probably be attended with fatal Consequences.' The petition was granted and a date in April was fixed for the visitation. William Hunter, a mason and wright in Kilmarnock, and John Duncan, a glazier there, were invited to provide technical assistance and all the heritors were to be informed and invited to be present.

The meeting took place on 17 April at Newmilns[99]. Mr Fawside, through illness, was unable to come out of his house to attend, but he was represented by Mr

Hill, a member of the Session. Mr Arnot, the factor of the Earl of Loudoun, reported that the Earl's absence, (he had been 'long from home serving his Country'), had caused delays, as everyone had been waiting for his return. The Earl had written a month earlier before 'he knew of the appointment of the Presbytery **to pull it down this Summer**'. As a result of this letter, the heritors had met and arranged to obtain tradesmen's estimates for **the rebuilding of the church**. He also suggested a slight delay until he could return home and 'because Timber was just now very dear and scarce'. In the course of the deliberations of these previous actions, some criticism must have been directed against Mr Fawside, as Mr Hill felt that he had to speak up in his defence.

Again estimates were asked for from the tradesmen a) of 'the expenses of repairing the church in the same size as it is' and b) the cost of major alterations 'because it is very low and some heritors desired that the walls should be raised four feet higher' and to bring in a separate Report how much the heightning of the walls will cost and how much it will cost to raise the Earl of Loudouns Isle in proportion'.

Consideration of what was to be done to the manse brought up a number of problems[100]. The heritors pointed out that in 1708 (neither Presbytery nor kirk session records survive for this period) there had been a presbyterial visitation and money was forthcoming for repairs to the manse and office houses. Again in 1724 the manse was repaired and enlarged at Mr Fawside's request, at which time he had agreed not to ask the heritors for any further money for repairs during the remainder of his incumbency. Also about

1736 the heritors, 'out of favour', had rebuilt the stable, brewhouse and cellar. They therefore claimed that any further costs should not be borne by them. In addition, they had five tradesmen check out the condition of the manse, etc., the previous week and they found that 'the manse and office houses being in disrepair is entirely owing to their not being duly thatched'. Unfortunately Presbytery records could not be found to confirm or deny the heritors' claims. Mr Fawside, through Mr Hill, indicated that he could not remember any such agreements and that 'suppose these things were true, he is not obliged to Rebuild the houses nor to furnish Timber and Stone or repair the Tear and Wear of them, that in the meantime the Houses must be inspected and repaired, and that this cannot be delayed without Danger of their Lives.' He did come up with a suggestion – 'if the heritors pleased, instead of repairing the manse and office Houses, to give him the Interest of a Thousand pounds Scots for hiring a House during his life, he would acquiesce in it'.

The tradesmen reported that the rebuilding of the church would cost £139 10s 2d sterling, if it was raised no higher than at present, but if it were raised four feet higher it would cost a further £17 2s 2d sterling and that the raising of the Earl of Loudoun's Isle would cost about £16 sterling. Mr Arnot said the the Earl would meet the cost of that part of the rebuilding himself. At the same time, it was reported that the repairs to the manse would cost £8 15s 4d.

At the next meeting of Presbytery on 12 June Mr Arnot reported that he had been in touch with the Earl of Loudoun, who was still in London[101]. The Earl had in his hands three different plans of a kirk and asked the Presbytery to wait till he arrived home so that a proper plan might be drawn up. The Presbytery felt that this request was reasonable and agreed to await his return. Mr Arnot also said that, with regards to the manse, he 'had made some offers to Mr Fawside, or his children' but Mr Fawside had not suggested anything, indeed had not even contacted him. The Presbytery therefore delayed discussing work on the manse, until their next meeting 'betwixt and which Mr Fawside will perhaps have made up matters with the Heritors'.

On 1 January 1751, the Committee which had been appointed to meet with the Earl of Loudoun reported that thay had met and that the Earl 'promised to have the Church of Newmills repaired or built with all expedition'[102].

It seems unlikely that if the church had been built in 1738 it would have been in the condition described by Mr Fawside. Not only that the fact that the Earl was considering three plans for a new building also militates against the 1738 date.

During all this time it is clear that Mr Fawside's health was deteriorating. The Presbytery appointed other ministers to undertake his preaching responsibilities. On 7 January 1752 Mr Adam reported that he had supplied Newmilns and the elder from that kirk 'applied for further Supply because of Mr Fawsyd's frail Condition'. This was provided[103].

Having served the parish for fifty seven years, Mr Fawside died on 10 January 1752, and his charge was declared vacant[104].

The years of Mr Fawside's ministry had been marked by changes of far-reaching importance for the people of Loudoun. Newmilns had become one of the main handloom weaving centres in the southwest of Scotland and boasted an annually elected Council of fifteen councillors, including a chancellor, a treasurer and two bailies. In 1739, the impressive new council house or tolbooth, with its fine double stairs at the front was erected. At first floor level was the meeting room and underneath the vaulted cellars, ideal for storage or prisoners. In the bell tower, the bell, it is said, bears the date 1547 (now illegible). If correct, could this be the bell of the old Lady Chapel, removed at one of the chapel's rebuildings or renovations?

The Jacobite rebellions of 1715 and 1745 came and went with little local impact, though the congregations of southwest Scotland were strongly opposed to the Jacobite Pretenders. The 3rd and 4th Earls of Loudoun commanded sections of the government forces during each rebellion.

John, the 4th Earl, 'the father of agriculture in this part of the shire', succeeded his father in 1731. It was he who transformed the entire landscape of Loudoun through the enclosure of his lands, the draining of the fields, the rotating of crops and planting a vast number of trees. As farm leases came to an end, the old farm units and fermtouns were regrouped and new farm units created with the tenants installed on nineteen year leases. The old rig system was abolished. The former division of land into infield and outfield was abandoned and more land improved for cultivation. The enclosure of the farms and subdivision of land into fields, marked out with thorn hedges and ditch boundaries, created the patchwork appearance of today's countryside. The Earl also constructed a road from Loudoun Castle to Newmilns, the first made road in the county, and built a substantial bridge across the Irvine. He established the small communities at Alton and Loudounkirk and initiated the development of Darvel as a separate village by granting twelve new feus for the construction of several cottages at its centre.

On the day that Mr Fawside's death was announced to the Presbytery, the Presbytery also received a proposal from the Earl of Loudoun about the minister's glebe[105]. He pointed out that the glebe was situated between two pieces of his land and as he was in the process of enclosing his land, it would be to the advantage of the minister and himself to exchange similar areas to bring his two parts together. Indeed the piece offered by the Earl was four falls larger and the Presbytery committee who inspected it declared that the ground to be acquired by the minister was of better quality. The Earl also agreed that he would clear the farm buildings of Hardhill and make the ground fit for cultivation. A peat road through the Earl's ground was to be created for the use of the minister. The houses at Burnmouth, occupied by James Dykes, were to be disposed of by the Earl and the growing timber in the north yard of Burnmouth, valued at £4 sterling, was to be sold off later, unless the new minister wanted to pay for it. And so the deal was done, and within a short time the dykes marking off the Earl's land were under construction.

On 14 July of the same year, Mr Arnot, acting for the Earl, presented Mr Andrew Ross, a probationer in the Presbytery of Stranraer, to be minister of Loudoun. The problems of patronage, however, were still aggravating the Presbytery.

'The Moderator upon this in name of the Presbytery, and in his own name, protested that this Church have alwayes reckoned patronages and presentations as a grievance and that they are of the same mind And particularly they protest that this presentation shall be but prejudice to the Rights and priviledges of this Church settled by Acts of Parliament and confirmed in the Articles of the Union betwixt Scotland and England'[106].
There followed the usual long, drawn out appointment procedures of the Presbytery.

Mr Andrew Ross, minister

Despite the encouragement of the Earl for the Presbytery to get a move on, nine months later Mr Ross was still successfully delivering his Exegesis in Latin for them on the subject 'Num satisfactio Christi sit necessaria'. It was not until 27 September 1753 that Mr Andrew Ross became minister of Loudoun, and a valued member of Presbytery.

It seems certain, although no mention of this is made in the available documentary records, that a new Loudoun Parish Church was built on the Newmilns site in the months after Mr Fawside's death and before Mr Ross's arrival in 1753. Indication of this is to be found in the detailed description of the ordination in the Presbytery of Irvine Minutes. According to normal procedure, the edict concerning the ordination having been publicised, the Presbytery was summoned by the kirk officer, James Richmond, to assemble at the church door. There they waited a considerable time and 'as none compeared to make objections against the Doctrine, Life and Conversation' of Mr Ross, the Presbytery resolved to proceed with the ordination and **'adjourned into the church'**. Thus Mr Ross had a new church to lead the worship in and, in addition, a refurbished manse in which to live in comfort[107].

Mr Ross's new church probably bore a strong resemblance to the one it replaced. Larger than its predecessor, it was smaller in all its dimensions than the present day church which replaced it on the same site. The walls were probably raised to a higher level than before to facilitate the creation of galleries. The interior was also similar, with the pulpit on the south side and beneath it the precentor's desk. One difference, however, lay in the accommodation of the congregation on pews in the central area. This church was not constructed with a steeple or bell-tower and the bell used for summoning the parishioners (not very effectively) was the bell hung in the belfry of the Town Council House.

During Mr Ross's ministry, his patron, the 4th Earl of Loudoun was overseas in the furtherance of his army career. In 1756 his mother, Lady Loudoun, sought the well wishes and prayers of the Presbytery and people of Loudoun in favour of her son 'who is going abroad to Command the Army in America for defence of the Plantations'[108]. His time in charge, however, was short. His command decisions came in for considerable criticism. He was recalled and then posted to Portugal as second in command of the forces there.

Mr Ross served the parish diligently until his transportation back to his home Presbytery of Stranraer, and the parish of Inch, on 14 September 1762[109].

Dr George Lawrie, minister

George Lawrie was presented to the parish of Loudoun by the Commissioner appointed by the Earl of Loudoun on 12 April, 1763 and duly ordained on 28 September[110]. He was thirty six years old and it was his first charge.

The new incumbent came from a long line of ministers. Several of his ancestors had served in parishes in Scotland and Ireland. His father, Rev James Lawrie, was minister of Kirkmichael parish[111]. George, born on 21 September 1727, was brought up in Kirkmichael and educated at the local school before leaving to study at Edinburgh University, aided in 1745 by a bursary from the Exchequer[112]. In Edinburgh he lodged with his married sister. During his time at university, his mother died. Perhaps his involvement in Edinburgh society proved too great a distraction and interfered with his studies, for although he had not completed his course and graduated, his father wrote to him in 1755 pointing out that he was wasting time in the city and being a burden on his sister. Accordingly that year he was licenced by the Presbytery of Edinburgh. His first attempt to obtain a charge in Ayrshire was unsuccessful. He applied for the vacant church of Monkton, but found himself in a patronage dispute between the Earl of Dundonald and Dalrymple of Orangefield. Both men put forward different candidates. George Lawrie's candidacy was supported by the Presbytery of Ayr, but an injudicious letter from the Presbytery to the Earl pointing out that it was the Presbytery's right to present caused such offence that the Earl gave the appointment to the other candidate[113].

Loudoun parish was perhaps fortunate that patronage did not appear to cause any serious grievance, in contrast to the contemporary situation (1764) in Kilmarnock. There, when the Earl of Glencairn presented Mr William Lindsay to the vacant charge of Kilmarnock, a general riot ensued. All manner of missiles, which had been stockpiled for the occasion, were thrown at the patron and the members of Presbytery. The Earl of Glencairn was struck on the cheek with a dead cat. Within the church, all was 'riot, noise and disorder'. In fright the Fenwick minister fled home on horseback. Mr Lindsay's ordination did eventually take place – but in Irvine[114].

An unknown biographer provides a mixed and not altogether flattering view of the new appointee: 'George Lawrie was a Moderate, a high and dry old Tory in politics, and without enthusiasm in religion. I think of him as a man of a good deal of humour, of literary tastes, and with much refinement of mind, and a most kindly nature, disposed to help. But he was lazy and never did any kind of work'[115]. It is clear, however, that he was relishing the prospect of his ministry in Loudoun. The Rev James Robertson, minister of Ratho and a close friend, wrote to Lawrie on 14 January 1765, 'I rejoice with you most sincerely on the happiness of your new state, much have I heard of the comforts of Matrimony but yours exceeds all I ever heard. Your declaration, even after the honeymoon, that three days at Newmills afford more happiness than an Eternity in another place is very high'[116].

At the start of his ministry, Rev Lawrie appears to have been satisfied with the physical state of his church, erected just before the incumbency of his predecessor.

Loudoun manse, however, which had been repaired and prepared for his coming was probably not very different from the manse at Kirkmichael in which he was brought up. 'The manse, like most of the minister's dwellings of those days, would be thatched, with a kailyard in front, the little narrow windows half-glazed, giving dim light through walls three feet thick to the low chambers and four rooms which were divided by wooden partitions'. In the house, there would also have been one or two serving women 'as active in the byre and the field as in the kitchen' and a man, who lived above the byre and who, as well as cutting and carting peats from the moor, 'has to look after the garden and the glebe, to plough, to reap, to thresh corn, and fodder the cattle'[117].

That same year 1765 brought two events had great impact on his personal life. Firstly his father, who had had such a great influence on his early years, died in August and then he himself, in late November, married Mary Campbell, third daughter of Dr Archibald Campbell, Professor of Divinity, University of St Andrews.

George and Mary Lawrie's family brought measures of pleasure and heartache. They lost their first child James, who was born on 30 September 1765 but only survived until 28 November. Fortunately they went on to have several more children. Twin daughters Christina (later married Alexander Wilson, bookseller, Glasgow) and Ann (later married Rev George Gordon , minister of Sorn) were born on 11 November 1766. Again Rev Robertson waxed lyrical on the births. 'If the man who produces Children singly is a useful member to the state, how invaluable a member of the Community must you be who are able to increase the number of His Majesty's subjects by Pairs. I'm disposed to allow you a great deal of Merit on this score but you must repeat the meritorious deed before your Character is quite established'[118].

It was now felt that the manse was needing too much work to be done on it and was becoming too small for the minister's growing family. A new manse was now built on rising ground overlooking the old manse and Burnmouth and beyond that the River Irvine. While the finishing touches were being made to the new manse, the family were accommodated in a house in Newmilns (later the Loudoun Inn). There another set of twins Archibald (who was to follow his father as minister of Loudoun) and Mary were born on 30 May 1768. Later in 1768, the minister and family moved into their new manse, known thereafter as St Margaret's Hill. The date of their arrival 1768 was carved above the doorway and in commemoration of the married couple the initials GL and MC were carved on the lintel over the entrance to the manse. In addition, the Hebrew words JEHOVAH JIREH (the Lord will provide) were inscribed separately. In their new home two further daughters came into this world, Louisa, born 31 October 1769, and finally Elizabeth, born 3 November 1772 but died 1 October 1773[119].

The surviving Minutes of the Kirk Session begin in 1759 and immediately illustrate in graphic detail the concentration of the minister and Session on aspects of moral discipline among the congregation, but at times there is also clear indication of the seriousness with which they approached other areas of their responsibilities. A topic which constantly exercised their minds was poverty and how to help the poor of the parish.

In 1765, the Sessions of Loudoun and Galston met with representative heritors to set out appropriate procedures in dealing with the poor, taking into consideration current legislation. The guidance document which they drew up contained seven points and to ensure proper conduct a copy was to be included in the Minutes of both churches[120].

1. Indigent Children may be Compelled to serve any of the Kings subjects without wages till their age of thirty years. Vagrant and sturdy Beggars may be also Compelled to serve any manufacturer and because few persons were willing to receive them into their

service, public work houses are ordained to be Built for setting them to work. The poor who Cannot work must be maintained by the parishes in which they were born and when the place of their nativity is not known that Burden falls upon the Parishes where they had their most Common resort for three years immediately preceeding their applying for the publick Charity. Where the Contribution Collected at the Churches to which they belong are not sufficient for their maintainance they are to receive badges from the Minister and Kirk session in virtue of which they may ask Alms at the Dwelling houses of the inhabitants of the parish.

2. The poor of both Parishes shall be maintained by that parish where they were born

3. In Case of a Husband and wife born in Different Parishes they shall be maintained by that parish where the Husband was born

4 When the Birth Cannot be acertained the maintainance shall be by that parish where that person resided Last three years

5. All Bastard Children to be maintained by that parish where the Child is born

6. The two parishes shall be mutually assisting to one another to get free of Burden of those persons who do not belong to any of them

7. And further for preventing of any differences that may arise with respect to the explication and application of the above articles they appoint as a standing Committee the Factors for the Time for the Earls of Loudon and Marchmont, the two Ministers and the two Treasurers of these Parishes for the Time being.

Another problem which Mr Lawrie had to face arose from differences within the population of Loudoun parish. For centuries the main occupations of the people had been connected with the land. More recently handloom weaving was becoming more and more prominent and associated with this was an increasing radicalism among the weavers. Newmilns too with its active Town Council was developing a strong civic conscience. As Mr Lawrie's biographer notes, 'In the course of his incumbency a large manufacturing village arose at Newmilns and a population of radical weavers grew up, with whom the minister had no sympathy and who cared not for the minister'. One outcome of this was the setting up in 1773 of a separate Meeting House just off High Street in Newmilns, for those who wished to worship apart from the parish congregation.

Another major event in George Lawrie's life was his meeting with Robert Burns. Lawrie's time in Edinburgh, so frowned upon by his father, brought him a wide range of personal friends and contacts among the major figures in the Edinburgh literary establishment. At the beginning of September, 1786 when he read Burns's 'Poems, Chiefly in the Scottish Dialect', he immediately sent a copy to Edinburgh to the famous Dr Thomas Blacklock for his appraisal and later the same month he invited Burns to his manse in Newmilns. The story of that visit is too well known to repeat in detail and proved of lasting significance. The welcoming atmosphere at St Margaret's Hill, the happy family life of the minister and the enthusiasm for literature, music and dance made a lasting impression on the poet[121]. Burns's response came in poetry written overnight ('Prayer –

O Thou Dread power'), a song ('The Night was Still'), a little inscription on a window pane ('Mrs Lawrie. She's all charms') and a lifelong friendship. Blacklock, in the meantime, as the first edition of the Kilmarnock Poems had sold out, was pressing for a second larger edition to meet the growing demands of a wider readership. And so Burns, at the end of November, took horse and set out to take Edinburgh society by storm. His Jamaica dream was soon to be extinguished, as his life moved on to a different path[122].

On 17 January 1791, George Lawrie was awarded the degree of Doctor of Divinity by the University of Glasgow and later that year his Account of Loudoun Parish was published in Sir John Sinclair's First Statistical Account of Scotland[123]. In his overview of the parish he was able to say that the structural condition of his church was sound and the more recently completed manse suitable for himself and his family.

On 1 August 1793, his son Archibald was ordained as his assistant at Loudoun, with a view to succeeding him in the charge[124]. The two ministers worked together for some three years, the son gradually assuming a larger role in the work of the parish.

The last meeting of the kirk session at which acted as Moderator and signed the Minutes was in 1796 and probably later that year he retired from Loudoun and took up residence in Maryfield at Greenhead in Glasgow, a house pleasantly situated overlooking Glasgow Green[125]. He died there on 17 October 1799, aged 72. His wife Mary outlived him by eighteen years, passing away on 23 January 1818 at the age of 88.

Dr Archibald Lawrie, minister

Born on 30 May 1768, Archibald Lawrie studied at Edinburgh University. It was when he was a student that he met Robert Burns, first in his father's manse, St Margaret's Hill in Newmilns, and then on a number of social occasions in the city. After his visit to Newmilns in 1786, Burns sent to his young friend a two-volume set of Macpherson's Ossian and a volume of songs to accompany a letter of thanks for the enjoyable stay he had with the Lawrie family[126].

After graduation, he was licenced by the Presbytery of Irvine on 18 January 1791 and two years later joined his father at Loudoun on 1 August 1793. As with his father, this was to be his first and only charge[127].

On 1 September 1794, Lady Loudoun's factor wrote to the Earl of Dumfries, who was looking after her business interests in her minority, alerting him to a problem that had arisen with regard to the church bell[128]. When the church had been last rebuilt, no steeple has been included 'to Hing the Bell for warning the people to Church'. The bell had been hung in the belfry of the Town Council House and now that belfry was 'falling down' and in need of urgent repair. He had two recommendations to make. Firstly, as the bell at the Town House was small 'not above 13 Inches diameter at the Brim and not heard at the extremities of the village unless the weather is calm', a larger bell should be sought like the ones on

Galston Church and other neighbouring churches. Secondly, hang the new bell in the repaired belfry and build a steeple on the church, transferring the new bell to the new steeple and leaving the old bell in the Town House belfry for the benefit of the Town and Council. He had costed the repairs at about £12 and a new bell at between £12 and £15, so that the whole job would cost nearly £30. The factor was of the opinion that the family of Loudoun would be happy to contribute their share of the work. The young Countess of Loudoun and her guardian must have agreed as the bell was immediately forthcoming. It hangs today in the church belfry. Its diameter is 20 and a half inches and bears the inscription 'FLORA COUNTES OF LOUDOUN . 1795'. Although there is no founder's mark on it, it may well have come from the foundry of George Watt in Edinburgh[129].

During his ministry, the Session records make no mention of the state of manse or church. The Minutes continue to record the constant stream of parishioners who had committed the sin of fornication once, twice, three times or four times, and who were seeking absolution. Occasionally one glimpses the other vital social work that the Session carried out. On 13 December 1795, Mr Lawrie reported that 'John Loudoun Weaver at Loudounhill died lately intestate and left a Widow and a Son of a former marriage and that this son is incapable to do anything for himself and likely to become a Burden upon the parish and it was necessary that the subject that belonged to the Defunct ought to be inventaryed for behooff of all concerned'[130]. Elders were appointed to see to carrying out the inventory and attending to the affairs of the unfortunate son.

The poor were always a main concern of the Session and we learn that on 7 February 1796, 'It having been mentioned to the Session by the Minister that the Charging of twenty pence sterling for private marriages in behalf of the Poor was attended with inconveniences they, to remedy this, and to increase the funds of the poor are unanimously of opinion that their Charge for private marriages shall be increased to two shillings sterling and it shall continue at this in all time coming'[131].

Archibald Lawrie married Anne McKittrick Adair on 2 April 1794. She was the sister of Dr James McKittrick Adair who, in 1787, had accompanied Burns on his tour to Stirlingshire and who married Charlotte Hamilton step-sister of Gavin Hamilton, Burns's close friend[132]. Their marriage was blessed with twelve children, eight girls and four boys. Their second child, George James Lawrie became minister of Monkton, their fifth, James Adair Lawrie became Professor of Surgery at Glasgow University, and their eighth Francis Rawdon Hastings Lawrie entered in to a successful military career. Ann Lawrie died on 12 February 1822 and ten years afterwards (12 January 1832) Archibald married Mary Howison, second daughter of John Howison of Holmfoot. Archibald and Mary had no children[133].

One resident of the parish during the ministries of the Lawrie father and son was Janet Little (1759 – 1813). Born in Ecclefechan, Dumfriesshire, in the same year as Robert Burns, Jenny went into service with Mrs Frances Dunlop of Dunlop, close friend of Burns, and later moved to Loudoun Castle to work in the dairy.

She won considerable local reputation for her poetry and in 1792 a collection of her works ('The Poetical Works of Janet Little, the Scotch Milkmaid') was published by J & P Wilson, Ayr. Robert Burns was one of the 700 subscribers. However, her efforts to win the friendship of Burns were rebuffed and he gave only lukewarm acknowledgment of her poetic ability. There is no indication how well her work was known to the occupants of St Margaret's Hill – she was a member of the dissenting Burgher congregation in Galston. Her remains, together with those of her husband, John Richmond, lie in the graveyard at Loudoun Kirk[134].

Archibald Lawrie was awarded the degree of Doctor of Divinity by Glasgow University on 14 March 1816.

He died on 5 May 1837. The Kirk Session Minutes make no mention of his passing. His wife Mary survived him by some 25 years.

Dr Norman Macleod, minister

A son of the manse, Norman Macleod was born on 3 June 1812 in Campbeltown, Argyll and lived there until his father was translated to the parish of Campsie in Stirlingshire. His student days were spent at the University of Glasgow and on graduation he was licenced by the Presbytery of Glasgow and presented by the Commissioner of the Marquis of Hastings to Loudoun Parish Church on 15 March 1838[135].

It was his first charge as a young minister and his first impressions gave him quite a shock. In a letter to a minister friend a few days after his ordination, he described the situation he found on his arrival[136].

'The parish is in a terrible state – very terrible! Its population is four thousand. The rural part is good and respectable, and so is Darvel ..... But Newmilns! What a place! Never, never, was there such desecration of the Lord's Day: dozens and dozens of lads walking about and trespassing on fields, and insulting the people and fearing neither God nor man! A large proportion of the population are born before marriage! The mass of the youth are sent to work before they can read, and in a few years are independent of their parents. In short, between drunkenness and swearing and Sabbath-breaking, the village is in a dreadful state – and may God have mercy on it! There is in all the parish an awful want of spiritual religion'.

But within a month his opinion was changing and on 7 June 1838 he wrote, 'I am very happy here, and I believe I may say that I and the people are the best of friends. I never received greater civility – the very voluntaries came outside their doors to shake hands with me. The church is crowded to suffocation – stairs and passages, and I never use a scrap of paper. I have an odd congregation of rich and poor, lords, ladies and paupers; but all sinners'[137].

It is clear that the young minister quickly determined where his main objectives lay. On 2 January 1839, in a letter to a friend, he set them out as a new church, an eldership, an infant school, prayer meetings, catechetical diets (to ensure better understanding of Scripture), an evening Sabbath class for young men and 'a tenfold greater strictness in giving admission to the ordinances' (to ensure that the congregation fully understood their responsibilities as church members)[138].

Early on Friday morning 10 January 1840, a messenger brought news of the imminent death of his patroness, residing at Kelburne, and a letter from her daughter, Lady Sophia, with a request. 'When my father died, he desired his right hand should be amputated and carried from Malta to be buried with my mother, as they could not lie in the same grave, as he had once promised her. His hand is in the vault at Loudoun Kirk, I am told, in a small box, with the key hanging to it. My mother entrusted you with the key of the vault, and begged you would give it to no one. May I request you to go to Loudoun Kirk and take out the box, and bring it here to me yourself…' The minister responded immediately and headed for Loudoun Kirk. In his own words, 'In half an hour I was in the dreary place, where but six months ago I was standing with Lady H beside me. When I contrasted the scene of death within, the mouldering coffins and 'weeping vault', with the peaceful morning and singing birds – for a robin was singing sweetly – it was sad and choking'[139].

His other parish work went on apace. In 1841, he completed a second visitation of Darvel and Newmilns (c.7000 people). Each week his Sabbath school catered for 600 children (10 till 11.30 a.m.). The main service was at 12 noon. His class for young men was held on Tuesday evenings. But his pleas to the patron and heritors concerning a new church appeared to fall on deaf ears[140].

To promote church order and discipline in the congregation and parish he devised a new set of regulations and recorded them in the Kirk Session Minutes on 22 July 1841. These included:

1. The Session shall hold an ordinary meeting on the first Sabbath of every month.
2. All persons desirous of being brought under church discipline shall appear before the Session at one of their ordinary meetings and intimate the same to the Session etc.
3. The Names of all such parties shall be read in the Church after public worship in the presence of the Congregation both when they first appear demanding and when they have obtained absolution.
4. All persons seeking the Sacraments for the first time in connection with the Congregation to intimate the same either personally or through an elder at the ordinary meeting of the Session.
5. All children baptized privately are to have their names made known publicly in the Congregation.
6. The Communion roll shall be examined carefully in Session sometime previous to each Communion that it may be purged of disorderly members and have new Members added to it.[141]

Two years later, in his campaign for a new church, he tried a different approach and arranged for a memorial (letter), signed by 193 members of the congregation addressed to him as Moderator and the other members of the Session dated 30th August 1842 setting forth the ruinous and dangerous state of the parish church and requesting the Session to bring the present state of the church before an early meeting of the Presbytery of Irvine. This tactic paid off. On 20 July 1843 the Presbytery met at Loudoun to examine for themselves the state of repair of the church[142]. Tradesmen who had been appointed to report indicated that the church was 'ruinous and unsafe for the performance of public worship'. Not only that the roof and galleries were in a dangerous state incapable of being repaired and should be instantly taken down. The windows were beyond repair and the walls were inadequate as a base for building on. The only option available was a new church, and it was suggested that the new building should have seating accommodation for a congregation of 1,200. As the tradesmen had provided no estimates of the cost of the construction, they were asked to submit these for a later meeting of Presbytery.

At his last Session meeting at Loudoun on 13 December 1843, Mr Macleod examined the Communion Roll and it was recorded that at 3rd December there were 842 communicants and 10 elders in the congregation. Even though it was his last meeting, he pressed on with his work, as he sought to tighten up the procedures for admitting communicants. For this purpose a guide for admission was drawn up and minuted. This entailed that:

‘All young communicants after having been examined by the Minister in private and having their names read over to the Kirk Session for their approval are admitted before the whole congregation generally the last day preceding the communion after having replied to the following queries:

1. Do you believe the Bible to be the word of God and the only rule of faith and morals?
2. Do you, convinced you are a lost sinner and that by the Deeds of the law no flesh living can be justified receive the Lord Jesus Christ as your priest and King and rest upon him alone for salvation?
3. Is it your intention and resolution trusting to Divine grace to lead a Godly life and adorn the doctrine of your Lord and Saviour in all things?
4. Will you be diligent in the use and outward means of grace in Prayer Reading and hearing the Word of God and partaking the Sacraments?
5. Will you endeavour to advance the Kingdom of your Lord and Saviour by your example, by your prayers and by your alms?’[143]

For the energetic Norman Macleod, Loudoun was only the beginning of an illustrious career. By the end of his ministry at Loudoun (1843), however, he had achieved a great deal. His church was now too small and structurally in a poor condition. Built to seat 800, it was incapable of coping with the number of communicants regularly partaking of Holy Communion (over 900). Through his efforts, the new building had been agreed and was being planned. But it would be his successor who would reap the benefit of his work. On 15 December 1843, Norman Macleod was translated to Dalkeith[144].

THE NEW LOUDOUN PARISH CHURCH

After Mr Macleod's departure, the planning work for the new church went on. The Presbytery and heritors agreed the estimated cost of £2067 4s sterling and awarded the contract to James Ingram in Kilmarnock, architect, William Anderson in Newmilns and Thomas Meikle in Strathaven, masons, and D and William Gemmel in Kilmarnock, Wrights, main contractors for the work. . On 3 May 1844, amid great ceremony the foundation stone was laid[145].

Mr James Allan, minister.

The Presbytery now began to search for a suitable successor to Norman Macleod. Several individuals were approached but none accepted the Call (one of these was Rev George James Lawrie, minister of Monkton and son of Dr Archibald Lawrie, Mr Macleod's predecessor at Loudoun).

On 12 September 1844, Mr James Allan who had been licensed by the Presbytery of Perth, was nominated and accepted the Call[146]. A man of wide experience, he had previously been a schoolmaster, an elder, assistant chaplain at Glasgow Prison. Thereafter he undertook the onerous duties of chaplain at Perth Penitentiary. Altogether he enjoyed a reputation of high character, conscientiousness and sobriety. He preached at Loudoun on 10 October to the satisfaction of the congregation and arrangements were made for his ordination on 19 November.

However, an objection, signed by six elders, was lodged with the Presbytery on 18 November and the ordination was postponed[147]. The Presbytery examined the 'libel' at length – Mr Allan had been seen in a state of intoxication in Perth and some of the local 'common strumpets' had tried to rob him of his watch – conduct which it was argued should disqualify him from being minister of Loudoun. Witnesses were sought and, despite having a letter signed by seven hundred of the Congregation supporting Mr Allan, the Presbytery found the accusations proven and Mr Allan was disqualified[148]. Mr Allan, however, appealed to the General Assembly, who overturned the Presbytery verdict[149]. His ordination took place on 4 July 1845[150].

During the vacancy, the ministers of the Irvine Presbytery provided pulpit supply and because the new church was under construction, services for the congregation, Kirk Session meetings and Mr Allan's ordination were held in the nearby Secession Church, with the agreement and friendly support of its minister, Dr Bruce.

The first service in the new church was held on Sunday 14 September 1845 and was conducted by the new minister, Mr James Allan[151].

POSTSCRIPT

As indicated in Part 1, no documentary evidence has been found to prove exactly when Loudoun Kirk eventually fell out of use. Maps of the 18th century show it as being in ruins. Its graveyard, however, remained in use until the 20th century. The burial vault, fashioned out of the chancel area of the old Kirk and now restored, continues to serve as the last resting place of the members of the Loudoun family.

NOTES

The merk = two thirds of £1 Scots = 13s 4d.

1 A&W Arch.&Hist.Coll. I, pp143-145
2 CSSR V, 1037
3 Acta Dom.Conc. (1501-1504) 352
4 Hendry, Part I, LK
5 Loudoun Chrs (DCK) Bundle 24, J394
6 Loudoun Chrs (DCK) Bundle 30, J475
7 Recs.Gen.Ass.Scot. p 316n
8 Turner, Memoirs pp 46,47
9 A.P.S. VI, ii, 138
10 Fasti (Second Edn.) III, 120
11 Scots Peerage V, 507
12 Donaldson, Scotland p.362
13 R.P.C. I (1661-1664) 292
14 R.P.C. I (1661 – 1664) 311
15 R.P.C. I (1661 – 1664) 321
16 Fasti (Second Edn.) II, 43
17 A.P.S. VII, 281, 282
18 Fasti (Second Edn.) III, 120
19 Donaldson, Scotland 368
20 R.P.C. II (1665 - 1668) 309
21 R.P.C. II (1665 – 1668) 351
22 R.P.C. II (1665 – 1668) 621
23 R.P.C. III (1669 – 1672) 18
24 R.P.C. III (1669 – 1672) 586
25 R.P.C. III (1669 – 1672) 590
26 R.P.C. IV (1673 – 1676) 104
27 Fasti (Second Edn.) III, 75
28 R.P.C. IV (1673 – 1676) 73
29 R.P.C. IV (1673 – 1676) 376
30 R.P.C. IV (1673 – 1676) 590
31 Fasti (Second Edn.) III, 59
32 Fasti (Second Edn.) III, 120
33 R.P.C. IV (1673 - 1676) 342, 343
34 R.P.C. V (1676 – 1678) 263, 264
35 R.P.C. V (1676 – 1678) 515
36 R.P.C. V (1676 – 1678) 541
37 R.P.C. V (1676 – 1678) 567
38 R.P.C. V (1676 – 1678) 423
39 R.P.C. VI (1678 – 1680) 177

40 Macintosh, Ayrshire Nights 156; Love, Legendary Ayrs. 219, 220
41 R.P.C. VI (1678 – 1680) 208
42 Donaldson, Scotland 371
43 Campbell, Witnesses 198-200; Love, Covenanters 72-74, 253-259
44 R.P.C. VI (1678 – 1680) 296
45 Love, Covenanters p. 18
46 Mitchison 78, 79
47 The Scots Worthies pp. 494 – 507
48 Mair, Newmilns p. 3
40 R.P.C. VIII (1683 – 1684) xviii, 60
50 R.P.C. IX (1684) 117; and R.P.C. XIII (1686 – 1689) 80-83.
51 R.P.C. VIII (1683 – 1684) 322; and R.P.C. X (1684 – 1685) 518
52 R.P.C. VIII (1683 – 1684) 328, 329
53 R.P.C. VIII (1683 – 1684) 346, 347
54 Fasti (First Edn.) II, 184
55 Pres.Irv. Mins. II, 9
56 Fasti (Second Edn.) III, 457, 458
57 Pres.Irv.Mins. II, 15
58 Pres.Irv.Mins. II, 26
59 Pres.Irv.Mins. II, 37
60 Pres.Irv.Mins. II, 39
61 Pres.Irv.Mins. II, 41
62 Pres.Irv.Mins. II, 45
63 Pres.Irv.Mins. II, 95
64 Pres.Irv.Mins. II, 15
65 Pres.Irv.Mins. II, 21
66 Pres.Irv.Mins. II, 30
67 O.P.R. (Loudoun) 603/1 Fr. 310
68 Pres.Irv.Mins. II, 136
69 Pres.Irv.Mins. II, 189
70 Pres.Irv,Mins. II, 27 Aug 1695
71 Pres.Irv.Mins. II, 197
72 Fasti (Second Edn.) III, 120
73 O.P.R. (Loudoun) 603/1
74 Pres.Irv.Mins. III, 444
75 Pres.Irv. Mins. III, 18, 21, 26
76 Dundonald Par.Recs. II, 584-591
77 Pres. Ayr, 31 Dec 1712
78 Pres.Irv.Mins. IV, 155
79 Pres.Irv.Mins. III, 44

80 Pres.Irv.Mins. III, 87
81 Pres.Irv.Mins. III, 40
82 Pres.Irv.Mins. III, 47
83 Pres.Irv.Mins. III, 253
84 Pres.Irv.Mins. III, 276
85 Pres.Irv.Mins. III, 80
86 Pres.Irv.Mins. III, 58
87 Pres.Irv.Mins. III, 115
88 Pres.Irv.Mins. III, 137
89 Pres.Irv.Mins. III, 385
90 Pres.Irv.Mins. III, 213
91 Pres.Irv.Mins. III, 218
92 Pres.Irv.Mins. III, 71
93 Pres.Irv.Mins. III, 129
94 Pres.Irv.Mins. III, 340
95 Pres.Irv.Mins. IV, 288
96 N.S.A. V, 834 – 855; also Strawhorn, Time of Burns 266
97 O.S.A. III, 106
98 Pres.Irv.Mins. V, 266
99 Pres.Irv.Mins. V, 272
100 Pres.Irv.Mins. V, 274
101 Pres.Irv.Mins. V, 284
102 Pres.Irv.Mins. V, 316
103 Pres.Irv.Mins. V, 365
104 Pres.Irv.Mins. V, 369
105 Pres.Irv.Mins. V, 369
106 Pres.Irv.Mins. V, 381
107 Pres.Irv.Mins. V, 432
108 Pres.Irv.Mins. V, 526
109 Pres.Irv.Mins. VI, 61
110 Fasti (Second Edn.) III, 120
111 Graham, Essays 138 – 160
112 Fasti (First Edn.) II, 185
113 Nat.Recs. Scot. GD 461/111, 3
114 McKay, Kilmarnock 115 – 122; cf. Galt, Annals 5
115 Nat.Recs.Scot. GD 461/111, 6
116 Nat.Recs.Scot. GD 461/112/7
117 Graham, Essays 139, 143
118 Nat.Recs.Scot. GD 461/112/12
119 Fasti (Second Edn.) III, 121
120 Loudoun Par.Ch.Sess.Mins. I, 15 September 1765
121 Mackay, Burns CL 127
122 Mackay, Burns Biog. 241

123 O.S.A. III, 63 – 69
124 Fasti (Second Edn.) III, 121
125 Nat.Recs.Scot. GD 461/111, 21
126 Mackay, Burns CL 127
127 Fasti (Second Edn.) III, 121
128 Loudoun Letter Book 59.
129 A.A.N.H.S. (Second Series) I, 237
130 Loudoun Par.Ch.Sess.Mins. I, 13 December 1795
131 Loudoun Par.Ch.Sess.Mins. I, 7 February 1796
132 Mackay, Burns Biog, 240, 241, 350
133 Fasti (Second Edn.) III, 121
134 Wilson, Little 4 - 24
135 Fasti (Second Ed.) III, 121
136 Macleod 80
137 Macleod 82
138 Macleod 84
139 Macleod 88, 89
140 Macleod 90
141 Loudoun Par.Ch.Sess.Mins. III, 22 July 1841
142 Loudoun Par.Ch.Sess.Mins. III, 20 July 1843
143 Loudoun Par.Ch.Sess.Mins. III, 13 December 1843
144 Fasti (First Edn.) II, 185; Pres.Irv.Mins. IX, 298
145 Newmilns T.C. Mins. Ayrshire Archives BNG 1/1/1/2
146 Pres.Irv.Mins. IX, 329, 331
147 Pres.Irv.Mins IX, 337, 339
148 Pres.Irv.Mins. IX, 363
149 Pres.Irv.Mins. IX, 365 – 372; Kilmarnock Standard 12 January 1946
150 Fasti (Second Edn.) 121
151 Hewitt 11

BIBLIOGRAPHY

A.A.N.H.S.Coll.	*Collections of Ayrshire Archaeological and Natural History Society* (Ayr, 1950 -)
Acta Dom.Conc.	*The Acts of the Lords of Council in Public Affairs 1501 – 1554: Selections from Acta Dominorum Concilii, ed. R.K.Hannay* (Edinburgh, 1932)
A.P.S.	*The Acts of the Parliaments of Scotland*, ed. T.Thomson and C.Innes (Edinburgh, 1814 – 75)
A&W Arch.&Hist. Coll.	*Archaeological and Historical Collections Relating to the Counties of Ayr and Wigton* (Edinburgh, 1888)
Armstrongs' Map	*A New Map of Ayrshire*, A & M Armstrong (AANHS Reprint, 1959)

Campbell, Witness	*Standing Witnesses; an Illustrated Guide to the Scottish Covenanters,* T Campbell (Edinburgh, 1996)
C.S.S.R.V	*Calendar of Scottish Supplications to Rome, 1447 – 71,*ed. J.Kirk, R.J.Tanner and A.I.Dunlop (University of Glasgow, 1997)
Donaldson, Scotland	*Scotland: James V – James VII* (Edinburgh History of Scotland, Vol. 3, Oliver & Boyd, 1965)
Dundonald Par.Recs.	*Dundonald Parish Records: The Session Book of Dundonald 1602 – 1731,* ed. H. Paton, 2 vols (Edinburgh, 1936)
Fasti	*Fasti Ecclesiae Scoticanae*, ed. H.Scott (Edinburgh, First Edn., 1848, Second Edn., 1920)

Galt, Annals	*Annals of the Parish*, John Galt (London, n.d.)
Graham, Essays	'Life in a Country Manse about 1720', in *Literary and Historical Essays,* Henry G Graham (A & C Black, London, 1908)
Hendry, LK, Part 1	*The Parish Churches of Loudoun and their Clergy up to 1845, Part 1. Loudoun Kirk,* Alastair Hendry (Friends of Loudoun Kirk, 2012)
Hewitt	*Loudoun Old Parish Church, Newmilns (1845 – 1945): A Centenary Sketch of the History of the Church,* E.T.Hewitt (Newmilns, 1945)
Loudoun Chrs. (DCK)	Loudoun Charters, Mss. held in the Dean Castle, Kilmarnock, now in Ayrshire Archives.

Loudoun Letter Book 59	Ms. Held in Ayrshire Archives.
LoudounPar.Ch. Sess.Mins.	Loudoun Parish Church Session Minutes, retained in possession of the current Kirk Session.
Love, Covenanters	*The Covenanter Encyclopaedia* (Fort Publ., Ayr, 2009)
Love, Legendary Ayrs.	*Legendary Ayrshire: Custom, Folklore, Tradition* (Carn Publ., Auchinleck, 2009)
Macintosh, Ayrshire Nights	*Ayrshire Nights Entertainment,* John Macintosh (Kilmarnock, 1894)
Mackay, Burns Biog.	*A Biography of Robert Burns*, James A. Mackay (Alloway Publ., 1992)
Mackay, Burns CL	*The Complete Letters of Robert Burns*, James A. Mackay (Alloway Publ., 1990)

McKay, Kilmarnock	*The History of Kilmarnock*, Archibald McKay (2nd Edn., Kilmarnock, 1858)
Macleod	*Memoir of Norman Macleod, D.D.*, Rev. Donald Macleod (London, 1891)
Mair, Newmilns	*The Pictorial History of Newmilns*, James Mair (Darvel, 1988)
Mitchison	*Lordship to Patronage: Scotland 1603 – 1745*, R. Mitchison (Edinburgh, 1990)
Nat. Recs. Scot.	National Records of Scotland, Edinburgh.
Newmilns TC Mins.	Mss. held in the Ayrshire Archives.
N.S.A.	*New Statistical Account of Scotland, Vol. V* (Edinburgh, 1845)

O.P.R (Loudoun)	Old Parish Registers (Loudoun) 603/1, microfilm in Local History Section, Carnegie Library, Ayr
O.S.A.	*The Statistical Account of Scotland*, ed. Sir John Sinclair, 21 vols. (Edinburgh, 1792)
Presb.Irv.Mins.	Presbytery of Irvine Minutes, held in National Records of Scotland, Edinburgh (CH2/197/-)
Recs.Gen.Ass.Scot.	*The Records of the Commissions of the General Assemblies of the Church of Scotland (1648, 1649)*, eds. A.F.Mitchell and J. Christie (Scottish History Society, Edinburgh, 1896)
R.P.C.	*Register of the Privy Council of Scotland*, Third Series, ed. J.H.Burton and others (Edinburgh, 1877 -)

Scots Peerage	*The Scots Peerage*, ed. Sir J.B.Paul (Edinburgh, 1908)
Strawhorn, Time of Burns	*Ayrshire at the Time of Burns*, ed. John Strawhorn (AANHS, 1959)
The Scots Worthies	*The Scots Worthies*, John Howie, ed. WH Carslaw (Edinburgh, 1870)
Turner, Memoirs	*Memoirs of his own Life and Times (1632 – 1670)*, Sir James Turner (Bannatyne Club, 1829)
Wilson, Little	'Janet Little and the Burns Connection', Agnes M Wilson in *Ayrshire Notes 41, Spring 2011* (AANHS, 2011)

ACKNOWLEDGEMENTS

My research has been made easier by the kind support of a great number of individuals, who made available documents in their care for me to study or provided information when requested. My thanks are due to

Sheena Taylor, Elaine Docherty and Tom Barclay, Local History Section, Carnegie Library, Ayr
Linda Fairlie and Bruce Morgan, Museum Officers, Dean Castle, Kilmarnock
Agnes Wilson and the Friends of Loudoun Kirk
Robert Miller, Session Clerk, and Roger Perry, archivist, of Loudoun Parish Church, Newmilns
The staffs of the National Records of Scotland, Edinburgh, Strathclyde Regional Archive, Glasgow, Dick Institute, Kilmarnock, University of Glasgow Library
Dr Christine Ewing, archivist, and her staff of Ayrshire Archives, Ayr and Kilmarnock
Robin Urquhart, archivist, and his colleagues, Thomas Thomson House, Edinburgh

The Loudoun material, held in the archives at Mount Stuart, Isle of Bute, could not be consulted as the archives there have been inaccessible for a number of years due to expansion, renovation and cataloguing of additional acquisitions.

Loudoun Kirk near Galston, Ayrshire, Scotland
Scottish Charity Number SC 023836

Web site: www.loudounkirk.org
Wiki: http://loudounkirk.wetpaint.com/

www.ingramcontent.com/pod-product-compliance
Ingram Content Group UK Ltd.
Pitfield, Milton Keynes, MK11 3LW, UK
UKHW020236250726
13967UKWH00001B/391

9 781291 173215